Common Prayer

FIONA SAMPSON has published fourteen books – including poetry, philosophy of language and studies of writing process – of which the most recent are *The Distance Between Us* (Seren, 2005) and *Writing: Self and Reflexivity* (with Celia Hunt; Macmillan, 2005). She has been widely translated, with eight books in translation including *Patuvachki Dnevnik (Travel Diary)*, awarded the Zlaten Prsten (Macedonia). She has received the Newdigate Prize, writers' awards from the Arts Councils of England and Wales and the Society of Authors and, in the United States, the *Literary Review*'s Charles Angoff Award. 'Trumpeldor Beach' was shortlisted for the 2006 Forward Prize for best single poem. She was educated at the Universities of Oxford and Nijmegen and has a PhD in the philosophy of language. She was Arts and Humanities Research Council Research Fellow at Oxford Brookes University in 2002–5. Fiona Sampson is internationally recognised for her pioneering residencies in health care and contributes to the *Guardian*, the *Irish Times* and other publications. Her translations include Jaan Kaplinski, an anthology of younger Central European poets, and *Orient Express*, of which she was founding editor. She is the editor of *Poetry Review*.

FIONA SAMPSON

Common Prayer

CARCANET

First published in Great Britain in 2007 by
Carcanet Press Limited
Alliance House
Cross Street
Manchester M2 7AQ

A CIP catalogue record for this book is available from the British Library
ISBN 978 1 85754 942 3

The publisher acknowledges financial assistance from Arts Council England

Typeset by XL Publishing Services, Tiverton
Printed and bound in England by SRP Ltd, Exeter

For J.P.

If I could catch the feeling I would: the feeling of the singing of the real world, as one is driven by loneliness and silence from the habitable world.

Virginia Woolf

Is it our job to disguise the black God in the sheep's clothing of the Good Shepherd Eros?

Jacques Lacan

Acknowledgements

Acknowledgements are due to the editors of the following: *Ambit*, *Ars Interpres* (Sweden), *Atlas* (India), *The 2007 Forward Anthology*, *Fulcrum* (US), *The Liberal*, *Literary Review* (US), *Magma*, *New Literary Review* (US), *New Writing 15*, *Poetry London*, *nthposition*, *Poetry Review*, *PN Review*, *Sou-Wester* (US), *Stinging Fly* (Ireland), *The Wolf*; and, for publications in translation, of: *Die Brüche* (Klagenfurt), *Gendaishi Techo* (Tokyo), *Helicon* (Tel Aviv) and *Nashe Pismo* (Skopje).

'The Plunge' was commissioned by BBC Radio 3's *The Verb*, 'Fog-bound' by Bath Literature Festival and 'The Miracle Cabinet' by Cambridge University Hospitals NHS Trust, who also published some of these poems as a chapbook, *Setting the Echo* (2005). 'Trumpeldor Beach' was shortlisted for the 2006 Forward Prize. 'The Looking Glass' and 'The Earth-wire' received *The Literary Review*'s Charles Angoff Award. I am grateful to the Arts and Humanities Research Council and Oxford Brookes Poetry Centre for a Fellowship in the Creative and Performing Arts in conjunction with the Wellcome Archive of Refugee Clinicians' Testimony.

I am very grateful to Charles Bainbridge, Ruth Fainlight and, especially, to Tim Liardet.

Contents

Messaien's Piano

Messaien's piano
throws notes like handfuls of stones
to clatter
against a glass-
house God:
        birds'
arrhythmic hearts,
they're precipitated into the bluster
and terror of spring.

The beautiful world hardly responds
yet these go on – chorus, soloist. *Make a joyful noise*
unto the Lord.

Are you glass –
your absence a mirror?
                Well, I lob stones.
Far off,
as from a distant copse,
hear what bodies do:
suspension,
interruption.
That long, perfect fall.

The Looking Glass

for John

Be mindful of that lovely blade you have fashioned; it is love and not a scourge.

St Umiltà of Faenza

Darkness at the window
                    holding your reflection,
a desk-lamp turning its bowl of warmth
onto the table

and here's your face,
its pale
          shield
blurred at the edges

so pallor moves out from nose, cheekbones, forehead
through streamers of dark hair
into the night –

whose pressure of something-else
is against your scalp
                    like a halo,
or that blue line
which oscillates
round a silhouetted face:
almost-sonar.
                    Trace
of the leverage
self exerts on its surroundings,

a message
needing the oscillograph's
                    fluttering wing –

though you understand disturbance
when a table-leg stops your shin,
                              or a voice
coming in under the umbrella light
breaks this skim

on concentration that's both here
and absent-minded.

★

            The room smells of coffee, aired linen:
a blur of pleasure,
           reassuring
as skirred light
caught in spirit photographs
where young widows of the Great War
saw themselves accompanied
through the dust
        beside a studio aspidistra,
into whatever was to come.

You lean forward,
wanting to stretch this moment –
to feel pleasure warm you

like the last time you were held face-to-face:
blurred eyes
        in the half-dark

and the way you felt
both in yourself and in them –
              seeing,
taking on form.

★

Or does this in fact have to do with language?
The way it hooks, draws in,

every name
        a displacement?

The nib in your hand's a crochet-hook
pulling things across,
          making starry combinations;

and if you've lost the knack, other generations
will move your fingers –

like that woman knitting on the Tube,
her hands' flicker and pass, flicker and pass:

                                        so familiar

you had to look away
from what you remember,

had to let her go
with the swollen faces in the ads sliding behind her.

And here it is again:
a mute, spatial awareness

of how things are,
                        unlearnt, unearned;
its grammar

something understood
before you stepped into the lights

and strange seeping-away clatter
of the Underground.

Edgware Road, Regent's Park,
                              Marylebone –

wayside shrines
on your journey in the dark.

                        ★

Diagonal, mineral,
the grain in glass
is a secret mark of grace –
you look through it,
see something flawless, thickening to white
only at the cut.

Leaning against a wall
at the foot of the stairs,
a sheet of glass
absorbs shadow
                        bottomlessly.

Its rim's a pool,

darkened colour
floating
        deeper than image
on polished struts and limbs of crystal –
light reflecting itself
endlessly, inward.

                    ★

In the dark beyond the window
March stirs: scat

of earth-smell,
                snowdrop spores
among the shadows.

It's a shift of the retina, of the chemical
membrane

            remembering, turning outward;
self's blurred frame –

opening
        in strange mimicry
of the window's arm that rakes out darkward –

a thickness like glass, where light could
                                        slip
nebulous
        nothing more than a glimpse;

as the rumoured big cat
runs the high *maes* of Cwm Elan,

absolute black
burning through those grasslands.

Now you remember
their attenuated glow
                    against dusk

where echo-lines of further ridges –
wave after wave –

lifted each minute,
holding it to the light.

A Sacrament of Watering

She appeared between lilac bushes.

)White snap of wings(

You knew she was there
by the quality of space whiteness of light:
even before she was there
                              she was there
endlessly
            this too a moment of light this too
a question of particles   clotting

the white of meaning
stilled in the familiar.

Meanwhile sensible-insensible enormous hands
pay out ropes and ladders of it

wide open   )light(O
paying out stains of yellow and blue
the horizon of colour.

There's such a thing as care, there is
a sacrament of watering
– she raises a hand
over the bent flags of pear –

her green breasts appearing among leaves,
her feet narrow as rays.

Pelted with leaves, the spilt leaves, in a blond storm:

white-throated   she's the wren

look, her long throat upturned she picks up mites,

her beautiful
              mute mouth.

                    She is

a spilling and pouring
the leaves in a pouring line, grass pushing up

returning   )movement of transformation(that bluer green
which the alder, taking on, spills upwards yellowly into blue.

She is
the stretched line of attention holding itself,

breath stilled.

Hay-on-Wye

Slim as a nun, I lie along
the margin of a borrowed bed
whose springs are texting, through my bones,
Abandon hope. Abandonment –

ecstasy of fall. I gaze
up into a godless dark
as if it might disclose some way
of getting right back, to the start

of that unselfconscious wish
for (old-fashioned diction…) *joy.*
And dark stares back. True, I'm pissed
again. But will the old alloy

always split along these seams –
is this, then, what incarnation means?

Trumpeldor Beach

Glimmering and vast
Matthew Arnold

Water breaks brightly
on sand –
a rhythmic
        exhalation,
then the delicate downward raking
through a scree of shells;

salt–blisters bloom between your toes
like the blossom of foam

gathering,
        dissolving
the edge of pure glare
silked here
        with ocean pink and blue.

Through each pale colour
you can almost see light
        itself:
filamented waves. Each pulls its dot of pigment
up to the brink of your eye
and back,
      a to-and-fro
of smudge,
        reflection –

Your glimpsed lash is like a fault in the view-finder,
a shadow of your self
        falling
through the sky's
        widening lens.

Now spool back
down this sequence of markers – self, lash –
to a molecule
trembling
       on the brink of becoming you.

It hangs inside you
                    moment by moment,
its painstakingness
millions of years old;

and this flushes through you
like a change in temperature –
an understanding that you're at the mercy
of chains
            and chambers
of water.

★

They float in the membrane,
mercurial. Adhering,
                    shifting –
you're occluded one moment,
the next
            open
to biting molecules of air;
challenge
and relinquishment.
                    One moment after another
taking you up
            and dropping you –

as if there can be no rest
for this splay-fingered bodily apparatus,
doggedly deliquescing
and refiguring
                    (mucus, blush,
pressure on a kidney),
with which you convert water to light.

★

Standing in smart clothes, holding your shoes clear,
you make the sea a radiant screen

sometimes suffused with shivers,
or stretched tight as skin

21

over itself:
a screen for the beach-room

you've lived in since childhood;
the roar your ear inhabits.

Easy to exchange an elephant-hide Atlantic
for this mercurial Med,
                            this dazzler,

whose urgent narratives from the middle of the world
slur against your bare feet –

a salad of old rope,
Coke tins, the parted armaments of bivalves.

From the cafés,
a smell of onions charring

as if the vivid sea itself
                            were burning them.
The fold and collapse of water,

like a hundred deckchairs,
is a cheerful lie.

              Water
always pressing towards water

as if it could dissolve the skin of the known world.

                       ★

The modern city,
                  tremoring against an early-morning sky,
sending itself upward in delicate
                            white flames behind you,
is hallucination.

It shifts in light
the way water
                  shifts a gleam from place to place –
spreading a myth

in which water combusts.

These are the fictional angels,
these bursts of supra-natural radiance
you could put your hand through;
that melt
        at the shadow of your foot
when you try to step in
to accept their cold
brilliant baptism.

                Coins of shadow
shift in puckered water.
Always this intermingling
as of strands within streams
rolling over each other; as of stone over stone,
rounded on each other
                but indissoluble.

In the valves and ventricles of your own body
are shadow
           and deep red luminescence,

the ghost of another country
rolling against light,
                among the shipping lanes –

floating towards some notional horizon.
A slur of light on water.

Take, Eat

Kissing and praying? Not the same.
Though each jaw, if it moves,
mumbles at a catch to prove
feeling. Capitalised Name

or nipple raised to Upper Case –
that taps your palate, jinks a toast
in soft communion – the boast
you mouth's the same in either case:

I'm yours alone. Nothing else
could mar my devotion. Self,
ambition, fall away here. See,
my praying mouth vouches for me –

Over and over. The lips part.
In shy darkness they lie, they gasp.

Common Prayer

Because even though he be stronger than the entire world,
he nevertheless is not stronger than himself.
                                    Kierkegaard

Streamers of willow
sough —
        grave, elastic —
in today's long-drawn-out Westerly;
this oceanic roar
blowing since the start of something
                                    far off,

carrying language you hear
but can't grasp,
                struggle
and give;
the revelation of scale
as it moves through the local.

Wind in the dead grasses of the paddock
a trace
        of the global, rim
of the driven planet:
contested, wrought.

                Screen-iron of sanctuary
and communion rail, in a dark church;
a hassock rasping bare knees.
Struggle. Prayer as continuing failure.
The self
        mounting by questions
to collapse —

        God
was in His own unbridgeable
distance.
Your fingers palpated your eyelids,
starring the red,
                a firmament of gold.

25

A pine coffin–cradle
rocked and murmured –
no wood is ever dead –
as you floated
in waters of sound.

                    That voice
testing the palate of the void
                              was yours;

alone among the congregation
echoing each other,
                    cut off from you,
from each other

as dark thickened the glass
of coloured windows.

It's not about belonging. You don't *belong*.
It's about the landscape
as confessor.

                    In the light-box of this pane
the white-branched willow moves to and fro,

spirit
        brushing the lens
of yellow-and-blue April,
                              its petalled fall
of what can never be concluded.

Impossible to emulate
the unaccountable give of growth.

But think of the Church as, say –
this umbrella.
Canvas stretches over its parts
like the silk of skin on ribs
                              that lift, shudder
and fall

in deep sleep:
                    the cute octagon of coloured nylon

26

suddenly at work,
all strain and counterbalance,
when the haft shoots up the handle
firing its butterfly wing at rain.

Afloat,
it tugs your arm higher,
                    a suggestion of levitation.

You are the arm. As you're the ribs,
fine graphite forced in a descending curve
by your own weight.

Rain streaks fugitive air.
A rainbow opens, so high
its near foot
seems vertical.
                If such brightness
walked the earth –

it's this monumental upright
                        the gale implies
with danger and buffeting;
not a father's
never-believed-in return

but the sought-for bridegroom
privately alight
                with recognition
in the garden.

Feral, generous –
maybe a shudder of wings –
keeping you company
while you remain awake,
moment by moment,
watching shadows of willow-twig
on a wooden wall:
                play
you never catch hold of –

the sift of branches
in April sun.

Body Mass

Each bone's a chalice: each gleaning thigh
a high-lipped cup. Understand –
desire's nothing personal.
Its sip and gulp, its search for why

he's on his knees before it, performs
a kind of private liturgy
for itself. He's asking *why* –
but not of you. Not of your bones,

which pour themselves between these sheets
of skin with practised cool. His cries,
his sticky martyrdom, belie
how it's a local godhead that he meets:

how, chasing flights of angels, he
tumbles to earth himself – in *we*.

The Earth-Wire

for Saso

*Depleted Uranium is ... primarily an alpha particle emitter
with radioactive half-life of 4.5 billion years.*

Gert G. Harigel

A cut in the pine-forest
above the Brogynin road:

the new clearing cluttered with piles of sawdust
stumps
       shining clods
dissevered timber,
            like battle playthings
of a Forestry Mars and Venus.

Round the pitch worn by their encounter, undisturbed,
blades of winter grass, groundsel,
mares' tails
in perfect miniature.

               You climb the seeping slope,
smelling pine –
sharp as a wound.

Spit pools under your tongue
like the woody taste of steroids
in sweat;
       and now woods return
as if everything can be mended,
as if pine-needles
can knit it back together.

Shadows drawn up in each direction
are shifty
       with the future-perfect of loss;

each triangular branch
outlining its own disappearance –

The sparse light steals these effects
as it makes them; fugitive,
                    a haunting
like the penumbra you cast
in the dim aisle.

★

The electrician finishes his cigarette,
tapping it into a sink

at the window, where every tone of *glas*
in trees and fields

opens a dry-point perspective.

Coming to the work, his giant's fingers
manage a threading, a netting of the earth-wire

you fail at:
your hands slip, burr on these tools

as dust clogs a blade's bite –
that intimate spiral
                    through studwork

which thuds the drill
back against your palms, your shoulder.

The house-pelt of wood dust is *nature mort*;
softens and dresses stone

and plaster the lathes slip through –
sibilant, flexible

as a memory of living wood
or the returning shadow –

when the sun moves west –
drawing a line under chairs, shelf, feet.

★

Scratched with snow-leavings, a slope
unbends millennia
                    as the train passes

to disclose furrows, pen walls,
                              a farmhouse
four-square against the plunge of contour:

the sort of place you imagine
meaning become daily,
                      like prayer,
in thick-walled rooms shadowy with life.
Brass ornaments,
                a *Farmers' Weekly* almanac,

the March light pooled on linoleum
or in the glaze of a mug;

things unalterably themselves

as if the death already in a man,
that fairground skellington,
didn't sticky each kiss.

                    *

Strata on mineral strata,
story connects what's half-seen,
half-imagined.
              Another day
you might see violet haze above a copse
as a place-marker;
as comfort
heaped like soil against your spade.

Story sifts down,
                  its fine grit
connecting this, to that, to you.

At dusk, though,
                airbase Apaches
thunder over these low, water-land hedges.
In darkness, you remember

the weight of a sick body
on your body;
                    too-ready sweat
its poison-ballast.

No need to pull these things together,
to lift them out of difference.

Day blurs beyond the doorframe
and real presences
ground
          what flickers in you:

just as in science class,
when you did the Copper Sulphate experiment,
their adamantine patterns
are taking root
                    ceaselessly
on wire.

The Plunge

Grace is the law of the descending movement.

Simone Weil

A cry bursts like a wing-beat:

among clicks and whirrs of language
your voice comes and goes.
Scraps from a hospital bed.

Is this our destination?
It's called a journey,
but you're not looking for something –
don't want to arrive
here
        in the cubicle dark
there
            at the end
beyond the night-lit corridor.

At dusk, mist rises from the river.
The green ball
in the drip-feed
lets only a little
pass.

We're going to the very edge,
to the darkness
where windows float their little boats.

Your illness is a kind of pact;
to bear it
is to bear even death
in this name – *love*.

Past midnight, I lean against the wall
to let a trolley pass.
It's always the same face on display,
twin cheekbones raising the skin
like tent poles,
your nostrils

dark
with the promise of air.

This is the river we dream about and dread.

Once, we saw an eel
caught by a heron,
the bird drinking it down
as if it were a black river.

Listen –

rippling polished lino, here it comes,
the wound
in the corridor's throat –
your shout
bursting the darkness open.

The giant listening on my tongue
swells
            with the sound,
I walk a corridor
as if there were something to count,
as if tiles spelt clues
                        or numbers:
they slide away
behind me.

Even as I tighten my hold
you're disappearing.
You telescope into your own black centre.

Is this it?
            All the love-feast
this salty
drip-feed?

The loneliness of your naked body
before the doctors and their equipment
uncovers me;
I feel the river's long
cold on my skin –

As you become unknown
even to yourself,
going on ticking and beating into the unknown
where you fight or yield, obey –
as oxygen detonates your lungs,
                    the catheter
milks your bladder –
or drown.

Is anything beautiful
left in the world?

You've placed fear on my finger,
ringed river-bird.

Draw the curtain.
Beds fill, empty and fill.
Is there any music to justify this?

Take me back to the midsummer river
hidden under brush –
that trickle of meaning.

Your fear
            and mine
make a verse with no answer.

Knee, hip, shoulder:
in the window's mirror
                    look
at the body
floating up
to the surface of night.

Anchorage

Those fasting women in their cells
drained a honeycomb brain
of every sugar drop of sense;
they made the skull a silvered shell
where love could live, cuckoo-like –

Would any question what she did
to distance her from how we live,
outside such dedication? – Shedding
the various world, so as to fit
in ways a jealous lover likes?

What flutters still is a bird: blown in
by accident, or wild design
of grace, a taste of something sweet –
The emptied self a room swept white.

Mehr Licht

Open the second shutter too, so more light can come in.

Goethe

But there's too much light
tremoring
        beyond vision:

aura of the concrete step,
of this door-handle
          you grasp
as you step away
from the slam of water into a sink.

Never mind. The windowsill's
                  a surprising red:
and you must ask yourself again,
this morning,
how to bear
        light –
spilling out of itself,
opening an interior
which is endlessly full.

Imagine the lotus.

Imagine nothing.
Here across the field come clouds,
carriers of rain and shine, moving
                    purposefully.
Here's your own translucent skin:
hold up this finger,
see how light makes a ghost of it,

silky with yellows and blues
streaming
to the vanishing point
             of future –

You bang the door behind you.

★

In the kitchen laboratory
always this struggle,
where things push against each other – resist,
marry.

      Along the table,
slipping from wall to floor,
will light just lay itself down in cellular instance,
green, brown;

will it strip itself out
in the shine of a plate?

Infinitesimal
          acceleration of cells
under the lenses
of soap-bubbles –
          Is this radiance?

★

The word you're looking for is
incandescence.

World burns: all edges and corners
burnished with leaf.

What you're afraid of –
pulling rays down into yourself
on the kitchen doorstep –
is that, secretly ignited,
          radiation
will transfigure you:

skin burn from your face,
gilded
     shelled with char,
your hair shrivel to a glowing pointillism,
your eyes
turn to glass,
        your tongue

a glitter of carbon
frost your mouth.

                            ★

At the sink,
when you run hot water
over glass already webbed with wet,
light refracts –

            a shadow
passing over the lens
with the whirr of migrating birds:
further, further,
they whisper

                  while
into the concrete L
between house and kitchen
sunlight flocks in a kind of Möbius wave
and return,
a continual pulse-less flow and exchange –
                                    look –

It's as if your palms are full
                        to overflowing
with water you can't cup loosely
or tight enough
                  to hold,

                            ★

you hold out your clumsy hands
                        in a blur
against the yellowish, slightly-damp
limestone of the lean-to

                  and *look*:
waves of colour-particles
are washing your hair, they're thrown streaming
down your back –
soundlessly
the whole scarf
of light; the pulsing crown.

In Carinthia

for Heimo, Brigitte and Elias

Beautiful it was to sit there, as in my skyey Tent, musing and meditating;
on the high table-land, in front of the Mountains …

Thomas Carlyle

Lunchtime. Take one of the green
metal chairs outside *Stand 17*, with Heimo, Brigitte and Elias.

The sunlight in the market place is mild,
as if outright warmth

would promise too much,
                              as if happiness
slips by

piecemeal and indirect:
                    Elias
staining his tongue on a lolly; streaks of twig

yellowed by spring sun along the Bahnhofstrasse
where a girl steps out a doorway –

her hair, with its lining of light,
a small annunciation

of everything she could be
or perhaps is.

              Your spoon clinks –
a chime among the city's bells

which rise like a charm;
and, rising palely at the end of the street,

local mountains press onward
                              continually –
spire after bright spire –

★

40

                        Step into the *Dom*,
past the gipsy-woman waiting at the door.
    Inside,
sunlight's muted by a brownish vault
where local saints raise themselves
towards an apex of mineral light
glimpsed through old glass,
                        a hem of blue
slipping away
            from their plumply outstretched hands;

they're all turbulent fabric
and thighs,
            celestial swimmers
kicking against stone and tempera:
what we want, closer to us
than what we see.

The frail eye blinks
                    in spills of brightness;
its yolk loosely stitched to albumen,
each blink fretted
                with dim stars –

while above, in a stainless sky,
pigeons wheel,
                a biplane
trails its storybook banner.

                    ★

The good life: always palpable.
The man in the next seat
                on the *IC Express*
isn't wrong when he says everything evolves,
life after life.

            He understands,
through all his
                reincarnation patter,
how each thing pulls inward to self –
catkin, white violet –
and toward each other;

                        41

hawthorn clouding hedges and embankments
a tree-spawn
          so sweet with pheromones
the nurses at the hospice used to say
it brought death indoors.

The man in the next seat
speculates
on this business of light
                    and sense,
body-work
building itself cell by cell –

a pollen of capillaries
brightens below your skin,
eye-lashes flicker,
               his breath's
dangerous vocative
is at your ear.

Important, then, to learn again
how much hangs on this:

the moment of decision
the lit thought –
                    brightening.

Important to understand the disciplines
of pink, *gemütlich* stucco,
washed sills,
well-ironed Viennese linen;
and of the labouring body
under its sheet
of skin.

          Obedience
to this given world,
whim after shining whim.

At the Sex Frontier

... the holy show
that models how the world should be
and could be, shared, glittering in near focus.

Les Murray

On a warm evening
breath and body-moisture
steam the glass,
making what should be clear
                              mysterious –
a blur of spoiled film.

But here I am, in Arrivals,
pressing my hand on the pane
to greet you.
                              When I take it away –
spy-holes,
a spatter of dots
clear as landing lights on the white surface;
and something I know must be you
shifting in them –
sleeve, eyebrow, wink of a button.

...Imaginary *noir*. Behind steam
you seem an emanation –
                              of the density of walls, doors,
surveillance cameras;
precipitated along corridors
with thunderclap footsteps and slams.

Meanwhile, water sets itself down
on convenient glass,
                              such as this pane:
stitch by plump stitch
tacking together hot
                              and cold –
which can't simply be folded
                              into each other
as if *this* were *that* –

My finger-holes spread and weep
in glittery water-mesh
which catches the outside world
and holds it back
          from this strip-lit foyer.

Obscurely *beyond*,
you're waiting for a kiss –
          semblable, frère –
but when I search the glass
I don't feel you. Only damp mineral shine,
dissolving cold.
        And yes, it's odd
to reach forward, cuff in fist –
making smears
         which fade like Döppler notes –
to where you hang
in the window's two-way mirror:

an icon on a screen
with your hand raised.

When your face
comes puckering up,
so that I lean across the shiny space between us
towards the image of me
floating in you
         like a palimpsest –

raising the banner of my lipsticked mouth –

it's to a familiar;
smudged blue and silver by these lights.

World Asleep

Darkness opens like a gate
again. My fingers on your latch
are tender when they lift the tongue,
slip a catch, then hesitate

across the entrance where you wait.
Your smile's a darkness joined to dark:
it widens as I close this gap –
almost noiseless. It's getting late:

nocturnal landscape – a country
I didn't choose – and I'm alone with you.
I kiss the soil. Its sweet reek
of straw's like longing, a snare of honey

to bite and bring me home to you:
a costly *heimat*. A world, asleep.

Blood Lyrics

from the Tokharian

1

They set our table under a tree.
I saw your hunger and was ashamed;

covered myself with words and silence
to break the line
from your mouth to mine.

Exile blackens your tongue with knowledge,
your black pupils are ravenous for my hunger.

Every day
in the oven of your mouth
you burn and raise me –
daily bread.

I taste of ash.
Eat me.

2

When you put your hands around my neck
I didn't know
whether I was large or small.

My bones flew out into the universe
and began to sing –

a scatter of small birds.

Did you kill me
or love me?

Night rises from the earth.

Always the same night
with its claws at my stomach.

3

You place your world between my teeth.
I take it with care –

this instrument on my tongue
beautiful steel.

Your words bridle me.
Where are we going?

Into pain that breaks
                        every bone in my face?

Moving your words
quietly, you fill my mouth with world –

bright, bitter coin!

The Archive

after the Wellcome Archive of Refugee Clinicians' Testimony

The street beginning to form he steps into it –
shopfronts composing themselves.

Zalewski outfitter's, Goldstein maker of walking sticks.
Cigars in the corner window mucus-yellow with age,
lucent glaze of gobstoppers,
                    all of it –
cold mornings, stab and jar of racing feet.
Latin, *golonka,*
ploughlines of a wet comb –

also certain words,
                  Porky, dirty Judas,
outside the pink-and-white torte of the church.

Father was In Carpets; import-export.
Even in the Depression, every Thursday at four,
pani Pawelska, little heels clicking, came with cash in a briefcase,
by the end it was a suitcase:
                  hard currency.

So – I went to Lvov. My parents paid.
You can't imagine it,
the marvellous life we had there
as medical students
            before the war.

In the cloudless summer of nineteen-thirty-nine
I came home
          for a holiday.

On the third of September
we boys stepped out the stunned houses –
Willi and Nix and I
with our bicycles like coffee-grinders –
and rode east.

Tracks,
       birch-groves,
once, the roar of a fighter from a fattening sky –

and shaky fingers touch steel, grip a handlebar,
your skin leaks sweat.
Moon licking the treetops.

By the fourth day,
                 eyes, ears, throat buzzing,
I saw death in trees, haystacks, the movement of water.

We volunteered at a field hospital:
wards full of the torn white strips of beds.

After a week the Russians arrived;
moustaches, boots, clamour of requisition.
And our officers,
             not exactly hostages,
their white dressings like feathers
we traded for civvies –

letting the kitchen door swing unattended, evenings.

Steel jumped in all the drawers
the night Nix and I and Willi
took our bicycles out into the dark.

      Breathe –
            good. And now – squeeze
      between lock and key:
      your secret thoughts neither Russian nor German.

We ended up back in Lvov.
Without money you make yourself indispensable:
days of queues, rumour, barter,
of hands cutting air,
            of bread and potato.
But even at New Year with *pani* Hubicka all milk and butter,
little Rosa's salt-meat tongue,

our parents' lives were
in the German shroud.

February.   Our bicycles lean together as if grazing.

Beyond yellowish grass
we can see the other Poland.

At dusk we move quietly,
willing the body to a quality of dark.
But in the fourth field a voice thrown up close by
is a startled bird:

Stop!

we stop

       Stop!

              but a shot sounds round us.
We raise our hands
            cautiously:
as if to move the air is to disturb it.

And so they line us up
empty our pockets –
               bootlace, pebble, penknife,
harmonica –
       Give us a tune!

Katya's little harmonica
at my mouth
like a cold lip.

I played a Russian song
and immediately the mood changed in the hall –
a requisitioned hall, surprisingly bright,
where the laughing commander says
So join us! In Russia, we pay your medical studies!

Our second time, it's also dusk.
                              Pig sheds,
pallets, straw. A propped spade.
A stranger squints from the porch.
                              He gets us across,
Willi and I wading the shocking current,
our bodies like sticks,
                    but Nix can't swim
Boys, I –

Where did he go?
            Afraid
                  back to the empty farm
                                    alone
and then? East to Lvov *in the middle of war,*
                              east to Moscow?

            I imagine him sometimes:
            an old man with his tea tray,
            somewhere in Russia.

When I came up our street and knocked the door my mother
screamed.
She thought we were both dead.
Strange. I had a brother.

They were very much reduced,
had no money.
            But Willi's father –

They were taking the young men, rounding them up
so Willi's father –
I was also blond. I could pass.
We would take film for the AK
and false papers.

            Why us?
                  Who knows –
            history's like that. Takes with one hand,
            gives with the other.

Night-trains. Endless bumping between sidings.
At Novi Sad a peasant eating bread and cheese
cut us crusts.
             At Bar we took the first boat –
coming in before dawn,
                     the death hour.

And Italy was hard walking;
                     fascisti everywhere.
In villages, faces pointed at us like suspicions.
A pebble could slip
the sheer flank of a hill
and peasants far below look up,
one of them with a rifle
raising rabbit-scuts of dust
by a stone cistern.

One time I took a ham from an outhouse –
its lover's weight under my arm.

Finally, in France,
the speeding, requisitioned train
station-masters at blurred attention;
in Paris – pale shocked streets –
                    the General
giving us to understand
              how *Very, very* –

and a Polish vessel slipping unlit
out of Vichy Marseille,
bound for Liverpool.

       As a doctor, so many slip through your hands.

Willi? Went in '44. On Fire Watch.
The warehouse
toppled stones on his grave:
                  who wasn't Jewish.
Willi, whose parents survived the war.

I wrote to them, enclosing his watch,
condolences and respects of the whole crew
a brave and very dearest friend.
                              Willi
might have stayed in Poland and lived
with his binoculars, thermos and lucky photo of Claudette Col –

We hadn't drifted apart it was hard we kept in touch.

Who saved my life. Whom I persuaded to volunteer.

Thresholds

Fish Market, Garrucha

The fish, when they arrived,
stood on their tails in lines.
Their skin was too many colours to choose –
changing from moment to moment –
but their eyes were fixed holes
where sea waited.

The men, all of whom knew fish
with the casual intimacy of husbands,
were so short
it was as if they'd been pulled downward,
an aquatic magnetism, towards the fish crates,
the sea below the dock.

In half-light, tourists assisted:
turning fish, men, into sea-monsters.

Poznań

Without our noticing
summer started to bloom between the clouds;
pollen stained the walls of buildings
above the tram stop.
The day was blowsy,
tipping itself
from the window onto my desk.
When a pair of climbing swifts
seeded the sky
and it began to thunder,
we got scared:
we took shelter under small tents
made of paper and poems.
Our nipples were roses.

Nocturne in Blue and Black

At dusk, a jeep drives this way, headlights
passing through the avenue of ash trees
business-like as cutlery on a blue plate.

Sky smudges the distance and the jeep merges
into blue dusk. The track under the headlights
corrugated. The jeep black, business-like.

At dusk everything is black and blue,
bruised by autumn, rain, the long night to come.
The jeep rolls along the track like a wind-up toy

and through the open window comes a smell of clay
and the lighter smell of drizzle in blue air.
The jeep passes black ash trees like forks

in a wide landscape. And the track's a knife,
dented and tarnished from over-use.
The jeep is small. Its headlights blacken the sky,

the track ahead and behind, fields turning to sky.
Even their clay is black, the spring wheat blue
under black sky. Headlights clatter across –

starting a hare. Later there'll be lamping.
Behind the jeep, ash trees shine in drizzle.
The blue fields and jeep go on into the sky.

Attitudes of Prayer

after Beethoven, Quartet in C# minor, Op 131

One hundred and thirty-one approaches
to the problem of God.
                    Imagine it:
over and over
rehearsing what you don't know,
soundlessly.

                    Letting yourself transcribe
what no one's said before –
in your greatcoat,
in the freezing study
where you take bitter tobacco, and coffee.

Occasionally, through the pall of tinnitus, hearing –
what?

        I feel as if heaven lay close upon the earth
and I between them both,
breathing through the eye of a needle.

Early December.
Grey on grey, grey annealing grey,

except light, catching the high
notes of a fiddle
(*quick quick said the bird*):
Your breath
like smoke on the window.

                    *

Light glints on a door-handle,
draws parallels on the carpet.

When you were a child
those voices in another room seemed far off.

Under the covers, in darkness,
you drew your knees up to your chin.

Lamplight on skin, on a polished table:
laughter lit up your mother's voice.

It made you think of honey;
                    slipped away
like the muntjac you see sometimes
browsing beyond the Service Station –

half-dog, half-deer,
caught on pause
            before neural pathways catch
and it flickers off
like something you can almost taste

but are afraid to;
let slip
            into shadows and trees.

                    ★

Light against dark. The way you remember Nazareth –
the cave-house
                    in the basement of its hanger-church

and the meal at a long table,
where the light from arched windows
was white
            and absolute,

each dish – a basket of pitta, long-leaved lettuce,
pastel swirls of hummus and tahini –
clear as a still life.

Night Fugue

1

Gathering left-over light, a barn owl
turns, pinkish wings
oaring strongly up
then lower:
turning at the end of each
disciplined row
displays
his wide human face then – on a twist –
sinks
in a heart-shaped plunge of white
splayed feathers
carrying light,
carrying the eye,
into long pale grass –

He lifts again almost backwards
onto dim currents;
the perfect chime of balance
in his wingspan
where light concentrates, a barium glow,
as if feathers are a print
of something hidden –

the body like music;
form opening through time
in a breathing line
a cry.

2

On the car radio, bell-like notes of John Cage
hang

as if there were no break
between you
and this somehow inexact nightfall;

between each hair
trembling on the leveret's back,

each compacted bud,
and the hum of your consciousness:

as if the unseen's primal halo
was unbroken
                by you.

Think of chimes falling on an anvil of air
that clangs back, upward –
                        each bell-stroke returned

to the echo-roof;
the wide Vale suspended

between breaths, between strike
                        and release.
Mile after mile of smudged black.
                        Think of yourself –

rapt velocity
tearing through the pulpy core of a spring night

as if towards an opening.
As if making a place through which

to close on *where-you-are-not*.
Like a pane of deeper dark in darkness:

something like that deepening of voice
when everything's seen between you.
                        You and it –

and hundreds of small, warm creatures
intent on this moment.

They go intently through you
towards daylight.

Mood-piece
after Verlaine

All the roses were red
and the ivy was all black.

Darling, that little shift you make
reawakens all my fears.

The sky was too blue, too tender,
the sea too green and the air too soft.

I always fear – this is what waiting is! –
you'll abandon me horribly

and I'm tired of the holly-bush with its glazed leaves
and the glossy box tree

and of never-ending countryside,
and of everything that isn't you.

A Second Look
after Heine

Honeysuckle − a summer evening −
once again we were sitting at the window −
the moon came out, animating, reviving −
but we were like a pair of ghosts.

Since we sat here together
twelve years have been crossed off;
meantime the heat of love, its great flame,
has died out.

I stayed silent.   But the woman
kept chattering, kept raking round
in the old love's ashes
− no spark −

and told a long story about how
she'd defeated bad thoughts,
how very shaky her virtue had seemed:
at this I looked unresponsive.

As I rode home, the leaves
of trees passed me in moonlight
like ghosts. Like a sad song −
but the dead and I, we ride fast.

The Dream of the Monstrance

Imagine a line, straining out
of dimming earth. Its vertical's
the unassuageable cry
desire utters when doubt,

always its double, conquers it:
like street lights, staining a spacious sky
invisible.
      Now – angle
your gaze along this, till you meet

whatever travels the other way;
some glint or catch, a give in night's
impassiveness – the whicker-flight
of geese. Promising you may

be lifted up; as by a Will
which comprehends your urgent call.

Scenes from the Miracle Cabinet

Teacher, my mouth is utterly unable to say what you are like.

Gospel of St Thomas

1

My metaphysic of presence –
that I am, *I am*
in the mirror
inside the miracle cabinet
        of the lift –

Leaving a fingerprint on the pane
        between *here* and *here,*
connecting and disconnecting
the world
        and the world of illness,
the look outward and the inward gaze,
        that array of glances
exchanged and dropped.

They hunt for the human,
for what secures us –
        the other
who sets up an echo in the self.

I called him but he gave no answer.

Rooms open beyond rooms –
their throats are flowers.

In secret chambers of the ward,
of the warded self,
I am pain's and pain is mine,
he feedeth among the lilies
arranged in chipped glass on a locker.

But I won't obey,
        each of us promises;
won't answer the body's
call.

Sun creeps across the window
and, in the fields, clods
turn naked flanks to it;
stunned, bruised.
In every bed a self, praying
Let it not be given to me
to understand suffering.

Is that your prayer
on my skin, like sweat?

I called him but he gave no answer.

A hundred keys to the human body
in a hundred drawers;

I'll open them all
until I find you.

2

Doors opening.

The sly music
                of the periodic table
enters your mouth.

Doors
        closing.

All of us naked
under coats, dressing-gowns, surgical scrubs;
the lift's giant balance tipping us
                                Going up –
into our incurable
selves.

Press your thumb in the cushion
of my palm.
                There –
that blanching,
there

at every touch:
the whole carnival springs to life
blood shooting through capillaries, urgent
pulses struggling
to diagnose your touch –

Level nine.

Hidden, your body becomes a refusal.
I should like to touch it
into pain – *Doors
                    closing* –

pain's nerve-lament.
Dark, voiceless music.

3

In the lift, a man
so covered with warts
it's obvious something terrible is happening to him
waits humbly, his blue-striped pyjamas
like a uniform of faith.
And God made man in His own image –
but we manage not to stand
exactly next to him.

Floor by floor and key by key, the lift
tunes the hospital.

Not every change is an upward modulation:
Who am I now?

You walk out in a new skin,
shining all over;
or end on a scaffold bed
among scraps of hallucination –

on this side of the fast, deep river
still asking the mortal questions:
Where are you?

From the pit of my bed
I sought him whom my soul loveth
and lo they came with
plastic water jugs, syringes, anti-nausea medication,
and I was not comforted.

                              To whom I said,
Saw ye him whom my soul loveth?
and they came with prick-tests for blood-sugar,
sleeping pills, bed-sore dressings.

But – I want the miraculous you.
Want the dry hand awkward
in my hand.
                  What else
trumps this necessary suffering,
alone,
            as the cubicle curtain
pumps in and out?

The watchmen that go about the city found me
to whom I said,
Saw ye him whom my soul loveth?

and they said
tick-tock, tick-tock,
time for tea.

Smoke trickles along the paper seams
of their roll-ups
and smells of you –

of your smoker's body,
which I want to touch
with all the artifices of compassion;
in which I want to touch
our common name.

And still
I do not touch you.

La Source

How does it start?
We know the end. The wide chute,
all of us toppled in the race;

arms, legs, feather of spume,
lips, kitten-heels, welcome
angle of laps. And the ocean roar

there all along
strumming the ear, carrying us,
coming back to greet us:

history booming beyond the sea wall.
We live tuned to this.
But it's not the start, this shore

where a man walking his dog
leans away from the waves,
leans to pick a pebble he chucks

into a wide-screen sky.
So, how does it begin? A lifetime away
in the green basin of a field

where a lens of rising water
bends the grass. Beyond the copse
rising again, uttering small sounds –

as a finch calls, bright, iterative,
from the fat-fingered alder beyond the ditch.
We can see the spot from the road.

That's it! you said. Streamers of tissue
under a stone, the worn path through nettles.
And I understood – this is the source

for you, the hidden spring. Our stories
carrying themselves from private origin
(this stone, its vein of glitter

parsable under your finger; this shank of thistle)
upwards and out – always outward.
They're what we share:

born again
to fall through lucid pools, the suck of sea.
But in late April when mud, warming,

snickers underfoot – here at the winterbourne
with its heartbreaking new cress –
this hand's my own; and what I touch with it

enters this story, *here*,
as a sign. As a contract
with this daylight; these local smells.

Fog-bound

for C.

Room after room
I hunt the house through
Robert Browning

Fogbound, the house
                drifts

towards a bluish distance,
where copses
stain the fog and pearl it.

Even the foreground's muted –
bramble, grass, willow–stem: flattened
as if colour
no longer carries a charge,
as if it were sound,

next door's car starting
in two dimensions
                of *tuh-tuh*,
the lorry on the road suddenly too close;

distance can't keep these things
in tension.

           Fog shields you –
it's a kind of caretaking
that reduces big questions
                to presence,

making you want to open the glass door
and step out
into its tall
           lightening.
A wateriness
lifting your hair.

★

The unknown is always arriving,
a continual rescuing flow round you
and on:

      fog's oozy bloom,
the pages of books –

their intimate, unconditional voices
all forgiveness when
shadowy
         below tall green walls
they fluttered off the shelves
into your hands.

Their leaves were soft, cool;
something opening
         as they flew open –

Already the dusty-boarded classroom
was being inked-out –
         blots on the sun –

Light slid across tables,
paint turned the water in the jam-jar milky,
olive-grey;
when you blinked, you saw red and gold
enamel your lids.

You could almost touch
what was spacious and vivid
as the sky beyond the windows

where tiny birds
looped in an Atlantic wind.

        ★

You long for what's spacious and vivid –
the unveiled mirror;

longing
      leading down perspectives of longing
the way temple floors at Plaoshnik on Ohrid
open into Byzantine colours
of pheasant and peacock

while below, on the afternoon shoreline,
reeds meal themselves yellow,
water crusts with glitter
               thrown out ceaselessly –
knots and fissures –
to the centre of the lake.

The slit of your traveller's eye opens
and shuts
at the shock of this.

★

On hot afternoons
dust visits the foyer of the National Museum

where the foreigner – awkward,
mute – pays double.

Behind the cashier
display-cases are turning themselves into mirrors,

light sibilates along them;
here, here it whispers,

smudgy with echo.

You press a finger on humming glass –

a deeper note rises through the hum
like its shadow,

as if your being here throws the switch
that lights-up the tableaux:

registering you they respond, dilate.
Alone in the gallery, you're blushing

with a recognition which seems
                              inauthentic –
too self-conscious;

but you want to slide out of yourself
into blacks, blues, reds,

the weight and swim of a geometry
familiar as your reflection.

★

Where to start from?

In the *Winterreise* bad weather makes a shroud,
fog binds the world
with cold-as-charity bandages.

Setting off
into the invisible, beyond music,
you strain at something
glimpsed –

but the retina's
all fog and shine,
light curtained by water.

How to catch what you're looking for
in the mind's
                    tricky lens?

Squinting
              in the exit's street-glare,
you remember ash twigs
held up for a moment against fog;

the way winter light slips
                              from room to room
of a house among water-meadows –

and how something was going ahead of you, always;
half-seen,
glittering,
as if crowned with water droplets.